The SANCTUARY for Lent
2013

Copyright © 2012 by Abingdon Press

All rights reserved.

No part of this work may be reproduced or transmitted in any form or by any means, electronic or mechanical, including photocopying and recording, or by any information storage or retrieval system, except as may be expressly permitted by the 1976 Copyright Act or in writing from the publisher. Requests for permission can be addressed to Permissions, The United Methodist Publishing House, P.O. Box 801, 201 Eighth Avenue South, Nashville, TN 37202-0801 or e-mailed to permissions@umpublishing.org.

ISBN 978-1-4267-4925-4
ISSN 0270-1758

Scripture quotations are from the Common English Bible. Copyright © 2011 by the Common English Bible. All rights reserved. Used by permission. www.CommonEnglishBible.com.

MANUFACTURED IN THE UNITED STATES OF AMERICA

ASH WEDNESDAY, FEBRUARY 13, 2013

Read Matthew 1:18-25.

This is how the birth of Jesus Christ took place.
—Matthew 1:18

Throughout Lent we will be exploring the life, teachings, and miracles of Jesus as described in the Gospels in the New Testament as well as their meaning for us today. We will begin with the birth of Jesus and conclude with the resurrection of Jesus.

Matthew and Luke describe in detail, with some variations, the birth of Jesus. Matthew's birth narrative centers more on Joseph than it does on Mary and does not go into as much detail or elaboration. Luke's birth narrative focuses more on Mary and the events surrounding the fulfillment of prophecy, along with the fact that Mary was a virgin both when Jesus was conceived by the Holy Spirit and born.

But it is only Matthew's Gospel that tells of the visit of the magi to the Christ child, Herod's massacre of children and infants, and the Holy Family's visit to Egypt.

References to physical birth and growth to maturity serve as metaphors for spiritual birth and maturation. When a person is born from on high and becomes a part of God's forever family, there is much cause for celebration. That event is miraculous too.

Prayer: Awaken me spiritually to new life and help me grow in my knowledge of—and love for—you. Amen.

THURSDAY, FEBRUARY 14, 2013

Read Matthew 2:1-3, 7-8, 11-12.

When they saw the star, they were filled with joy.
— *Matthew 2:10*

We really do not know who the wise men—or magi—were who traveled to Jerusalem looking for the one who had been born and was destined to become King of the Jews. They had seen a new star rising, and this caused them to believe that a great king had been born on earth. Because the star appeared over the land of Judea they assumed that this new king would be King of the Jews. So they went to Jerusalem seeking King Herod, since they believed that surely the present king would know the identity of any newborn king.

Herod had to consult his experts regarding the beliefs and traditions of his people and the writings of the prophets. He sent the magi to Bethlehem and told them that if they found the child to come back and let him know so that he could pay tribute to the child also. But, in reality, Herod was afraid of losing his powerful position and wanted to get rid of any newborn competitor for his throne. The new star led the magi to the place where the Christ child was with Mary and Joseph. Signs in the heavens above were agreeing with events on earth.

When the magi found the child, they honored him with gifts suitable for a king: frankincense, gold, and myrrh. What gift or gifts are you willing to give Jesus?

Prayer: Dear Jesus, I willingly give you whatever resources I have that can be used for your glory. Amen.

FRIDAY, FEBRUARY 15, 2013

Read Matthew 2:13-14, 16, 19-20, 22a-23.

Having been warned in a dream, he went to the area of Galilee.
—*Matthew 2:22*

How have you received guidance from the Lord? Did you pray and study the Scriptures? Did you get quiet within and seek to discern the Spirit's gentle leading? Did you consult a trusted spiritual friend, prayer partner, or your pastor?

When Jesus was born, people in those days believed that one of the primary ways that God made his will known to them was either through angels or dreams, or a combination of the two.

Scripture says that the Lord appeared to Joseph in a dream, warning him to take Mary and the baby Jesus to a place of safety in Egypt in order to escape Herod's massacre of the innocents. After Herod died, the Lord appeared once more to Joseph in a dream and told him to return to the land of Israel with Mary and the baby.

The Lord's guidance protected the holy family by allowing them to escape Herod's treachery and to find refuge in a foreign land until they could safely return home. God still seeks to guide and protect those today who are sensitive and responsive to the promptings of God's Spirit.

Prayer: O God, help me to be receptive and responsive to your guidance in whatever form it may take. Amen.

SATURDAY, FEBRUARY 16, 2013

Read Matthew 3:1-11.

In those days John the Baptist appeared in the desert of Judea announcing, "Change your hearts and lives! Here comes the kingdom of heaven!"
—Matthew 3:1-2

When John the Baptist emerged from the wilderness, he proved to be quite a controversial figure with his camel hair robe, the wide leather belt around his waist, the smell of the wilderness on his body, the fire of God in his eyes, and the even more fiery rhetoric that he used to challenge people to repentance and faith. His style, dress, and manner reminded the people of the prophets of old. He confronted the people with the immediate availability of God's kingdom and invited them to become a part of it. The way that they were to indicate their willingness to repent and become part of God's kingdom was by being baptized with water in the Jordan River.

To repent means to have a change of heart and mind, to begin expressing a new attitude toward sin and the salvation that comes from God. To repent means to stop living for self and to start living for God. Those who repent are more concerned about what God thinks than what other people think. God's will, then, becomes a top priority for those who repent and turn from their sins.

Prayer: Lord, this day I let go of my selfish and sinful ways, and I want you to be in charge of my life. Amen.

SUNDAY, FEBRUARY 17, 2013

Read Matthew 3:13-17.

Heaven was opened to [Jesus], and he saw the Spirit of God coming down like a dove and resting on him.
—Matthew 3:16b

At the time of his baptism, when Jesus came up out of the water, he saw the heavens opened, and the Holy Spirit came fluttering down like a dove and rested on him. Although the dove has been used in Christian art to symbolize the Holy Spirit, Scripture does not say that the Holy Spirit came down in the *form* of a dove, but in the same *manner* as a dove. The important thing is that the Spirit settled on Jesus, anointing him for his ministry. In the Old Testament, the Holy Spirit sometimes came on people, so they could perform a specific task. The Holy Spirit was consistently with Jesus throughout the entirety of his earthly ministry.

Perhaps what Jesus saw was perceived by spiritual eyes so that only the spiritually sensitive could see it. Other Scripture indicates that John the Baptist may have also seen this manifestation of God (John 1:29-34). But this experience and the affirmation of Jesus as God's beloved seem to have been primarily reserved for Jesus and perhaps for John.

Think of a time in your life when you have been truly enfolded by the arms of God and experienced God's amazing grace and unconditional love. How would you describe your experience to others?

Prayer: Let your Holy Spirit settle on me, informing and empowering my life for you. Amen.

MONDAY, FEBRUARY 18, 2013

Read Matthew 4:1-11.

The tempter then came to him and said, "Since you are God's Son command these stones to become bread."
—Matthew 4:3

Scripture refers to Jesus' being tempted by the devil in order to prove the quality and depth of his faith. Times of temptation or testing come to all of us, but they are not to be eagerly sought. With them comes the possibility of succumbing to the temptation or failing the test. That is why Jesus taught his disciples to pray "And lead us not into temptation." Temptation is something that we are to face reluctantly, but we must understand that there will be times when our faith is put to the test (4:8-9). Finally, Jesus resisted all of the devil's temptations and dismissed Satan with the affirmation that only the Lord God should be worshiped and served.

We often think of temptations that have to do with morals and ethics or the way we treat others. But the crucial temptations that Jesus faced had more to do with his core faith and values: his use of divine power, the temptation to presume upon God's favor, and the question of whether he was in charge or his heavenly Father was in charge.

Prayer: Lord, whenever I face temptations, help me rely on your strength and guidance. Amen.

TUESDAY, FEBRUARY 19, 2013

Read Matthew 4:18-22.

"Come, follow me," [Jesus] said, "and I'll show you how to fish for people."
—*Matthew 4:19*

When Jesus called his first disciples who were fishermen, his appeal to them was based on the nature of their vocation. In essence, he told them, "You men make a living by catching fish; but if you follow me, I will show you how to fish for and catch people."

God has a way of using our natural gifts and abilities to fulfill God's kingdom purposes, as well as for God's glory and our ultimate benefit. The farmer or gardener who knows how to nurture and grow crops may also learn how to nurture and grow people or churches. The police officer who guards and protects us from criminals may also become a spiritual guardian and protector of God's people. The skilled surgeon, who is able to save people's lives, may also help people to remove from their lives malformed spiritual tendencies so that they can be blessed and healed by God's Spirit. The comedian who makes people laugh may also be able to share his or her joy in the Lord and lift the spirits of listeners. The nurturing parent may also be able to nurture the spirits of others, help others grow in the Lord, and inspire them to do great things.

What interests and capabilities can you identify in your life that Jesus can use to glorify God as you seek to serve the Lord?

Prayer: Lord, show me the capabilities that I have that can be used to glorify and serve you. Amen.

WEDNESDAY, FEBRUARY 20, 2013

Read Mark 1:21-28.

Right away the news about him spread throughout the entire region of Galilee.
—Mark 1:28

When a person gets a new car, gets a job promotion, or buys a house, he or she can't wait to share the good fortune with others. Why, then, are we so reluctant to say a good word for Jesus at every given opportunity? Are we afraid of being misunderstood, ridiculed, or accused of being hypocritical because we may fail to live up to the demands of the faith in Christ with which we identify?

One of the most misunderstood problems that people in Jesus' time dealt with was that of demons or evil spirits that sometimes dominated people's lives. They could hear demons howling in the desert, and witnessed strange behavior that demons appeared to cause, as well as saw various physical illnesses attributed to demons. So when Jesus liberated a man from the influence of an unclean spirit and did this in a synagogue where he was teaching, this caused a great deal of discussion among people about Jesus' identity and the power of his teaching. As a result, news spread about him throughout the region.

What amazing signs and wonders has Jesus done for you that you could describe to others as a means of sharing your faith?

Prayer: Dear Jesus, liberate me from destructive attitudes and harmful tendencies. Amen.

THURSDAY, FEBRUARY 21, 2013

Read Luke 4:14-30.

When they heard this, everyone in the synagogue was filled with anger.
—Luke 4:28

According to Luke, when Jesus began his public ministry and sat down in the synagogue to read from the scroll of Isaiah, the text indicated that a time of renewal could be anticipated. But although the gracious words of hope that he took from Isaiah's text create a sense of wonder, the portion of the original text that Jesus withheld from his reading made his listeners angry. They were so angry, in fact, that they wanted to kill him. What he omitted from the text was a reference that Isaiah made to the vindication of Israel (Isaiah 61:3-9). This indicated that although Jesus was decidedly a Jew, his ministry was to be made available to all people, including Jews and Gentiles. He was not to be just Israel's Messiah but the world's Savior as well.

There have been times when a particular church or denomination attempted to claim exclusive rights to the salvation that Jesus offers. But such attempts are the exact opposite of the global availability that Jesus had in mind. No one group, denomination, or individual has a monopoly on the gift of salvation in Christ.

Prayer: Savior of the World, motivate me to share the good news of your salvation with everyone. Amen.

FRIDAY, FEBRUARY 22, 2013

Read John 2:1-12.

His mother told the servants, "Do whatever he tells you."
—*John 2:5*

When Jesus and his disciples attended a wedding feast along with his mother and perhaps other members of the family, Mary picked up on the fact that the hosting family had run out of wine. Given the importance that people in her culture placed upon hospitality and graciousness, for the hosts to run out of wine at a wedding feast would have been a source of great embarrassment to them. But Mary saw in this situation an opportunity for Jesus to come to the rescue, although she may not have anticipated the dramatic manner in which Jesus would respond.

At first Jesus gave Mary a mild rebuke for trying to push him into doing something about the situation. But Mary knew her Son. So she pointed out Jesus to the servants and indicated that they should do whatever he told them to do, even if it was something unanticipated. Jesus later told the servants to fill with water the jars used to provide water for the ceremonial washing of guests' feet, then get some of it out and take it to the headwaiter as if it were wine so that he could taste it. When the headwaiter tasted it, he pronounced that it was the best wine of the evening. He also commended the host for saving the best wine until last.

Prayer: Lord Jesus, whenever things go wrong, help me trust you to set things right. Amen.

SATURDAY, FEBRUARY 23, 2013

Read Matthew 5:1-11

Happy are people who are hopeless, because the kingdom of heaven is theirs.
—Matthew 5:3

In Jesus' introduction to what is commonly referred to as the Sermon on the Mount, he states that what is valued in God's kingdom is the complete opposite of what the world values.

The happy ones are said to be the hopeless, grieving, humble, and hungry; those who are merciful, have pure hearts, and make peace. Others described as happy include those who are ridiculed for living the way that God wants them to live, those who are insulted because they follow Jesus, and those who suffer persecution and are falsely accused.

The word translated as *happy* in most modern versions of this Scripture may not accurately convey its true meaning in some readers' minds. We tend to think of ourselves as being happy when we get what we want when we want it, when things are going our way, and when we are prosperous and successful. We should associate the word *happy* with the word *blessed*, which means "to be fulfilled."

The truly happy—blessed—are not those whom most people would expect. The happy—the blessed ones—are those who live in a right relationship with God.

Prayer: Heavenly Father, may my relationship with you bring me true fulfillment in spite of outer circumstances. Amen.

SUNDAY, FEBRUARY 24, 2013

Read Matthew 6:5-6.

But when you pray, go to your room, shut the door, and pray to your Father who is present in that secret place.
—Matthew 6:6a

Nobody knows very much about your prayer life unless you talk about it, write about it, or do a lot of praying in public places. The Pharisees made a point of praying in public places on the street corners where they could be seen by others. Jesus said that by doing this they had fulfilled their purpose. Their primary desire was to be seen or heard by others. This desire took priority over their desire to encounter God and be heard by God.

So Jesus said that it would be better to pray in private in a room with your door closed so that you could pray to the heavenly Father in that secret place. In that way your prayers would likely not be designed to impress others, but to contact and converse with God.

John Wesley took Jesus' teaching on prayer so seriously that he actually had a prayer closet built in his bedroom with an exterior window in it so that he could get up early each morning, study the Bible, and pray. He did this not to impress others but to nurture and fortify his own spirit. Where have you found a quiet place to pray so that you can be alone with Christ in your thoughts?

Prayer: Lord, help me to find a quiet place where I can intentionally be alone with you each day. Amen.

MONDAY, FEBRUARY 25, 2013

Read Matthew 6:7-15.

If you forgive others their sins, your heavenly Father will also forgive you.
—*Matthew 6:14*

One of the greatest challenges that we face in life is forgiving others who have betrayed, falsely accused, partially criticized, and ridiculed, hurt, or abused us in some way. And yet Jesus taught us that we must forgive others, expressing the same attitude toward them that the heavenly Father has expressed toward us.

Forgiveness does not mean that you no longer remember the injury that you have sustained from another. It means that when you think of that event it no longer raises your blood pressure, stirs your anger, or motivates you to seek revenge.

A retired minister was going on his morning walk in the park near his residence when a young man rushed up to him, put a pistol to his chest, and shot him in the heart. The minister died and the young man stole his wallet. But the perpetrator was caught, and at his trial the minister's widow testified, asking the judge to show leniency to the young man and not give him the death penalty. In a very dramatic and specific way she fulfilled the Lord's command to forgive others.

"I couldn't do that," you may be thinking. But you could if you have truly experienced God's forgiveness.

Prayer: Lord God, help me forgive others because you have so graciously forgiven me. Amen.

TUESDAY, FEBRUARY 26, 2013

Read Matthew 21:18-22.

If you have faith, you will receive whatever you pray for.
—Matthew 21:22

This is one of those crucial passages of Scripture that invites us to believe what appears from our perspective to be impossible. And yet we learn from descriptions in the New Testament that Jesus has a way of expanding boundaries of possibility for his followers.

Walking with his disciples and hungry, Jesus saw a fig tree and examined it for ripe figs, but there were none. So he cursed the fig tree and said that it would never again bear fruit. As a result, the fig tree withered and died. This must have astonished the disciples. But Jesus told them that if they did not waver in faith that they could cause even a mountain to rise up and cast itself into the sea. The lesson was that unwavering faith gets results. My guess is that the disciples never saw another fig tree or mountain without remembering what Jesus said.

Of course you and I have probably not moved any mountains or withered any fig trees lately. But we have probably witnessed the visible results of our faith or that of others whenever it is expressed.

Prayer: God of Love and Power, increase my faith and enable me to receive whatever I ask of you. Amen.

WEDNESDAY, FEBRUARY 27, 2013

Read Matthew 21:28-32.

"Which one of these two did his father's will?"
—*Matthew 21:31*

    Most parents can appreciate Jesus' story about a man who had two sons. The father asked one son to go out and work in the vineyard. But the son refused. He probably thought that he had better things to do. However, later he reflected on it, and he went out and did the work that his father told him to do. The father asked the second son to work in the vineyard, and he readily agreed to help. However, something else got his attention and he forgot the promise he had made to his father. Now Jesus asked the chief priests and the elders which son obeyed his father's instructions. They, of course, said it was the first son, the one who had initially rebelled against the father and eventually had a change of heart.
    Of course Jesus wasn't talking about any father or just any two sons. He was providing a metaphoric description of the relationship between the heavenly Father and the Jews and Gentiles. His point was that even tax collectors and prostitutes were responding positively to the call to have faith in Jesus, but many of the Jewish religious leaders were not. And yet ever before us is Jesus' call to repent of our sin and believe in him.

Prayer: Lord Jesus, help me repent of my sin and believe in you. Amen.

THURSDAY, FEBRUARY 28, 2013

Read Matthew 21:33-46.

Finally he sent his son to them. "They will respect my son," he said.
—*Matthew 21:37*

Today's Scripture relates one of two vineyard parables that Jesus told. In Jesus' parable about the vineyard owner and the workers, Jesus clearly wasn't talking about just any vineyard owner or workers. The workers in the vineyard were the Jewish religious leaders, the vineyard owner was the heavenly Father, and the vineyard owner's son was Jesus.

The somewhat veiled message was that those who rejected and even tried to destroy God's Son would be severely dealt with. That message is just as true today as it was when Jesus first said those words. Our ultimate fate hinges on our response to Jesus. Forgiveness and judgment are opposite sides of the same coin.

This parable demonstrates that Jesus was fully aware of who he was and how the Jewish religious leaders would respond to him. How have you responded to Jesus? Have you rejected him, ignored him, and sought to discredit or otherwise destroy him? It is not too late for you to express faith in God's one true Son so that you can experience forgiveness and salvation to eternal life.

Prayer: Lord Jesus, let my response to you be one of faith that trusts you more than anyone or anything else. Amen.

FRIDAY, MARCH 1, 2013

Read Matthew 22:23-33.

Jesus responded, "You are wrong because you don't know either the scriptures or God's power."
—Matthew 22:29

    It is possible to be thoroughly acquainted with the content of the Scriptures and still not have a genuine experience and solid commitment to the Lord of the Scriptures. There was a man who knew the King James Version of the Bible forward and backward. A Scripture could be quoted to him and he would tell the chapter and verse where it was located. He could be given the chapter and verse and he could quote it word for word from memory. The only problem was that his lifestyle demonstrated that he did not truly understand the Scriptures and had never had a transformative encounter with the living Christ.

    In order for us to be all that God calls us to be, we must have both knowledge of the Scriptures and the experience of God's power at work in our lives. The Pharisees and scribes of Jesus' day were well acquainted with the content of the Scriptures. It was the power of God that they had yet to experience in a personal manner. They knew that God exists out there somewhere, but they did not realize that God's Son was standing in their midst and was calling them to faith in him.

    The Scriptures are intended to call us to faith in Christ as well as facilitate our experience of Christ as a living and present reality.

Prayer: Lord Jesus, I believe in you regardless of the circumstances or the consequences. Amen.

SATURDAY, MARCH 2, 2013

Read Matthew 24:3-14.

Many false prophets will appear and deceive many people.
— ***Matthew 24:11***

Throughout history there have been false prophets claiming to represent God. Some appear to be prosperous and successful so that many people assume that God must be blessing them and approving of their actions. But in spite of their claims, they do not represent God.

A widow sent her entire Social Security check to a television evangelist, leaving her without the financial means to pay her rent or purchase food and medicine. When the church of which she was a member learned of her predicament, the pastor volunteered to cover her living expenses for that month. He admitted that his actions indirectly meant that his church was supporting the same questionable ministry to which she had contributed. But he also acknowledged that she was a child of God and a part of their faith community. This meant that they were duty bound to help her.

When he warned us about false prophets, Jesus was providing a word of caution and underscoring the necessity of being careful whom we trust to provide us with spiritual guidance and direction.

Prayer: Holy Spirit, provide me with true discernment in order to see the nature of my spiritual leaders. Amen.

SUNDAY, MARCH 3, 2013

Read Matthew 24:29-35.

Heaven and earth will and pass away, but my words will certainly not pass away.
—*Matthew 24:35*

We live in a world where many people are strangers to the truth. Being honest and keeping their word does not seem to be high on the list of some people's priorities. Although there was a time a person's word was his or her bond, even in those days there were people not keeping their word. But God is not like us. God can always be trusted to keep God's word and fulfill God's promises.

Not only does God intend to keep God's word, God has the power to do so. God created the heavens and the earth by speaking the material world into being. God's word is a creative word. Whatever God says comes to pass. This means that God can be trusted to accomplish whatever God says.

We do not need to remind God of the promises made to do certain things for us. But we do need to remind ourselves that God has made such promises. God's word remains true and dependable in spite of the circumstances. God is truly the Ultimate Promise Keeper.

God has promised to forgive those who acknowledge their sins and repent. God has also promised to judge those who refuse to repent. The choice of whether we experience forgiveness or judgment is left up to each of us to decide for ourselves.

Prayer: Ever dependable Living Word, remind me that you always keep your promises. Amen.

MONDAY, MARCH 4, 2013

Read Matthew 24:36-51.

Therefore you also should be prepared, because the Human One [Son of Man] will come at a time you don't know.
—*Matthew 24:44*

Most of what Jesus said about his Second Coming and the Day of Judgment had to do with being expectant and prepared. Those people who are found faithful will be rewarded with the gift of eternal life. Those who are determined to be unfaithful will face a terrible fate.

Those who have experience with sheep tell us that sheep are much more cuddly and willing to follow their shepherd than are goats. Most goats have a tendency to go off on their own. The sheep are more inclined to recognize the shepherd's voice and to come when he calls. This implies a relationship that the sheep have with the shepherd that expresses trust as well as dependence. Therefore when the shepherd separates the sheep from the goats, he is separating them on the basis of their nature or character as well as their performance. Although the shepherd may want to gather both the sheep and goats to him, he recognizes that they have different natures and different needs.

God's love is available to all of us but custom tailored for each of us.

Prayer: Heavenly Father, show your love to me in the way that I most need to experience it. Amen.

TUESDAY, MARCH 5, 2013

Read John 14:15-26.

"I won't leave you as orphans. I will come to you."
—*John 14:18*

    Throughout Lent we have been studying various events in Jesus life as well as some of his teachings. The story of Jesus is an active story with much drama, conflict, and action. But the story does not end with the Gospels. The Spirit of Jesus, or the Holy Spirit, continues through the apostles to teach, heal, and liberate people while the young church is being birthed and nurtured. The story of Jesus does not end with the establishment of the church or even the assembled writings of the New Testament. Jesus continues to lead, motivate, and empower his church today.
    Prior to his crucifixion and resurrection, Jesus told his first followers that he would not abandon them and leave them to their own devices. He would come to them through the Holy Spirit to provide them with everything they would need in order to faithfully serve him and tell others about him. The gift of Jesus' ongoing presence is the secret of the church's life and continued relevance in today's world. In Christ we have the reality of forgiveness, the possibility of new beginnings, and the promise of eternal life.

Prayer: Holy Spirit, motivate and empower me to serve God faithfully and to witness courageously the good news of Jesus Christ. Amen.

WEDNESDAY, MARCH 6, 2013

Read Luke 10:1-24.

Jesus replied, "I saw Satan fall from heaven like lightning."
—Luke 10:18

When Jesus sent seventy-two of his followers out to heal the sick and announce the arrival of God's kingdom, there was a sense of urgency about his message. When they began to be impressed with themselves for the way that they were able to command demons in Jesus' name, Jesus reminded them that Satan had fallen from heaven like lightning because he was overly impressed with himself. Then he said that they should be rejoicing in their relationship with God instead of their authority to command demons.

Legend has it that more than two hundred years ago evangelist George Whitfield traveled to Bath, North Carolina, in order to proclaim the gospel. Met with a negative response, he left that town and, in keeping with today's Scripture text, shook the dust off his garments in protest against the people and pronounced this curse upon the town: "May you never grow larger than you are now." The town of Bath, so the story goes, is still approximately the same size that it was when Whitfield visited it. Of course, that could be just an old legend with no historical truth to it. But it does underscore the fact that there is both power and a sense of urgency in the message of the gospel.

Prayer: Everlasting God, help me rejoice in my relationship with you and as a citizen of your kingdom. Amen.

THURSDAY, MARCH 7, 2013

Read Galatians 2:16b-20.

I have been crucified with Christ and I no longer live, but Christ lives in me.
— **Galatians 2:19b-20a**

Paul described his ongoing relationship with the living Christ in this manner: he speaks of being crucified with Christ, of Christ's living in him, and of living by faith—the faithfulness of God's Son, who sacrificed himself for Paul and for us all. He identified himself with the saving work of the Christ of Calvary, Christ the faithful witness and the sacrificial lamb, the Christ of the empty tomb, the Christ of the Emmaus road, and the Christ of the Damascus road.

Everyone who is born into this world is terminally ill. It has been said that to be born is to begin to die. Life on earth experiences disintegration to the extent that every living thing eventually dies.

But death is not the end of the story for believers. Our life before God continues. Regardless of whether we live or die, we belong to the Lord.

Prayer: Living Lord, keep me close to you so that whenever it is my turn to die I will continue to live forever with you. Amen.

FRIDAY, MARCH 8, 2013

Read Luke 12:13-21.

"After all, one's life isn't determined by one's possessions, even when someone is very wealthy."
—Luke 12:15b

A college student returned home at the close of his first semester of college and stopped by the local gas station to buy some gas. The attendant who knew him asked him when he came in to pay for the gas, "Did you hear about Mr. Flynn dying?" The recently deceased man was rumored to be the richest man in town. "How much did he leave?" the student asked. "He left it all," the attendant replied.

You really can't take it with you. When you leave this world you leave all of your material substance behind. You leave the money that you have accumulated, your investments, real estate, and cars, your jewelry, and even the clothes that you wear. The only thing that we take with us out of this world when we die is our relationship with Christ Jesus.

The quality of your life is not determined by how much wealth you have or how much money you leave when you die. What does it say about you if people profit more from your death than from your life?

Prayer: Lord, give me a spirit of generosity toward others and help me not put too much emphasis on material things. Amen.

SATURDAY, MARCH 9, 2013

Read Luke 12:22-34.

Don't be afraid, little flock, because your Father delights in giving you the kingdom.
—Luke 12:32

 The kingdom of God is not taken by stealth or storm. We cannot charge the gates of heaven and crash our way through. We cannot sneak unnoticed over the back fence. We cannot bluff our way through by pretending to be deserving of entrance into God's heavenly realm. There's no such thing as a valid counterfeit admittance ticket to heaven. The kingdom of God is not a goal that we achieve through hard work or a prize to be won, but is a gift to be received. The only way that we gain admittance is by knowing Jesus and being known by him.
 Being a part of God's eternal kingdom is not something earned as a reward for having lived a good life or for services rendered. God's kingdom is a gift that is extended to us that we are free to either accept or reject. It is not something that we earn or deserve. Citizenship in God's kingdom is a gift that we can receive even though we do not deserve it.
 Jesus taught his followers that the heavenly Father delights in giving us the kingdom. God is further delighted and all heaven rejoices when even one sinner lets go of his sin and embraces the kingdom that is given.

Prayer: Help me, Lord, to cease striving to earn the right to be a part of your kingdom and instead to accept your kingdom as a gift from you. Amen.

SUNDAY, MARCH 10, 2013

Read Luke 14:7-11.

All who lift themselves up will be brought low, and those who make themselves low will be lifted up.
—*Luke 14:11*

Renowned preacher, writer and missionary E. Stanley Jones was elected as a bishop in his jurisdiction while he was out of the country on a mission trip. When he returned and was informed of his election he refused to accept it, saying that he had a higher calling, which was to be a missionary.

This doesn't mean that all bishops who are elected should refuse to serve because they perceive that some other calling takes priority for them. But it does demonstrate how Jones sought to be sure that his priorities were aligned with God's priorities for him. He was such a humble man that even though millions of copies of his books had been sold, whenever he submitted a new manuscript for editorial consideration he always included a self-addressed stamped envelope in case the editor receiving it did not choose to accept it.

God can use each of us in a mighty way if we are willing to accept the role that God has in mind for us. That role may not gain for us a lot of public acclaim or financial prosperity, but it will be something that brings glory to God, affirms God's kingdom values, and can be used for our ultimate benefit, as well as serve to help others.

Prayer: Dear God, help me not think too highly of myself and give you the glory and the credit for the good things that you enable me to accomplish. Amen.

MONDAY, MARCH 11, 2013

Read Luke 21:1-4.

He said, "I assure you that this poor widow has put in more than them all."
—Luke 21:3

One night on television there was an advertisement for a widow's mite—a small copper coin in a white gold setting, complete with a white gold chain for $199. It was rather ironic that the seller had taken a small copper coin without any real substantive value and enhanced its value by placing it in a gold setting.

The value that Jesus placed on the widow's two small copper coins called "mites" had more to do with the attitude expressed by the widow than the market value of the coins themselves. This incident in the Gospels may provide the origin for the expression "putting in your two cents' worth." But it also reminds us that God does not look at things the same way people do. Jesus saw in the woman's meager offering an attitude of total trust in and devotion to God. As poor as she was, she wanted to do her part. Jesus recognized the true value of her offering even though it wasn't encased in precious gold. And that widow has been remembered in the Scriptures because of it. Those two small copper coins were worth a lot more than most people realized.

Prayer: Lord, help me give my all in devotion to you and not to measure my gifts by the amount of money that they represent but the amount of love in my heart. Amen.

TUESDAY, MARCH 12, 2013

Read Luke 18:18-30.

Jesus replied, "Why do you call me good? No one is good except the one God."
—*Luke 18:19*

When a certain ruler addressed Jesus as "Good Teacher," he may have simply been trying to show respect for Jesus or perhaps give him a compliment. But Jesus gave a different nuance to the man's form of address by asking him why he was addressing Jesus as good. Since God is the only one who is truly good, did this mean that the man thought Jesus was God?

Although we have no idea what was in the man's mind when he addressed Jesus in this manner, it did give Jesus an opportunity to affirm that ultimate goodness can be found in God and God alone.

The man had successfully and consistently lived up to the letter of the law. But his desire was to go the distance and do whatever was necessary for him to receive eternal life. So Jesus told him that he needed to sell everything he owned and give the proceeds to the poor and then come and follow Jesus. The man must have regarded this demand of Jesus as being insanely harsh. He went away sorrowful—he trusted in his riches more than he trusted in Jesus.

Who or what in your life do you trust more than Jesus?

Prayer: Savior, remove from me any burdens or distractions that threaten to hold me back from truly serving you and telling others about you. Amen.

WEDNESDAY, MARCH 13, 2013

Read Luke 18:35-43.

They told him, "Jesus the Nazarene is passing by."
—Luke 18:37

Jericho was a town that most of the Jews avoided because it was in Samaritan territory. Jews and Samaritans customarily did not associate with each other. Jews regarded Samaritans as unfaithful half-breeds who were not allowed to worship at the officially designated temple in Jerusalem and in retaliation had set up their own temple on a mountain in Samaria.

When the blind man near Jericho was told that Jesus of Nazareth was passing by in the crowd, he cried out for Jesus to help him and would not allow the people to prevent him from having access to Jesus. Twice the blind man addressed Jesus as Son of David, which is a title of royalty often associated with the Messiah. Jesus asked the blind man what he wanted; the blind man replied that he wanted his sight restored. So Jesus healed him by speaking a few simple words.

What do you want or need Jesus to do for you that only he can do? He can do exceedingly, abundantly far more than you have dared to ask or think possible.

Prayer: Lord Jesus, give me faith to reach out to you and help me trust as I seek your help that you will give me what I need in order to serve you and tell others about you. Amen.

THURSDAY, MARCH 14, 2013

Read Luke 19:1-10.

Jesus said to him, "Today, salvation has come to this household because he too is a son of Abraham."
—Luke 19:9

It's a favorite story of children in Sunday school. In Jericho a tax collector—a wealthy man—of small stature had to climb a sycamore tree in order to get a glimpse of Jesus as he passed by in the crowd. When he saw Zacchaeus in the sycamore tree, Jesus called out to him, "Zacchaeus come down at once" and suggested that they have a meal together. As a result, Zacchaeus happily welcomed Jesus into his home and pledged to give away a good portion of his possessions and to return four times as much to others he had cheated.

Even though Zacchaeus was despised by the people because he had used his position as a tax collector to cheat them, Jesus acknowledged that Zacchaeus too was a son of Abraham because he had been eager to welcome Jesus who embodied salvation.

It is not in our status or family heritage but in the way that we respond to Jesus that enables us to experience salvation to eternal life. How are you responding to Jesus? Do you trust him as your Savior, and are you seeking to follow him as your Lord?

Prayer: Dear Jesus, I already trust you to be my Savior and follow you as my Lord; by your grace deepen my ability to trust you and enable me to follow you more faithfully. Amen.

FRIDAY, MARCH 15, 2013

Read Luke 22:1-6.

Then Satan entered Judas, called Iscariot, who was one of the Twelve.
—Luke 22:3

No one really knows for certain why Judas betrayed Jesus. One simple explanation is to say that the devil made him do it. But as followers of Jesus, we are given the strength to resist the devil's influence. Some think that it was because of the silver coins that Judas was given in payment for his betrayal. From that perspective he is often believed to have been a very greedy person who would willingly sell out his friend for money. Others believe that Judas may have sympathized with the Zealots and sincerely believed that he could force Jesus into a situation where he would have to display his divine power in order to save himself and others. If that is the case, imagine how disappointed and alarmed Judas was when Jesus allowed himself to be taken captive by the mob and arrested.

We do know that Judas later attempted to return the money that he had been given and tried to make amends as best as he could. His sense of regret was so deep that eventually he hanged himself. Before we are too quick to judge Judas harshly, we might ask ourselves whether we might be capable of some form of betrayal of Jesus as well.

Prayer: Savior, help me not judge others too harshly, lest I be found guilty of committing the same sins that they have. Amen.

SATURDAY, MARCH 16, 2013

Read Luke 10:38-42.

One thing is necessary. Mary has chosen the better part. It will not be taken away from her.
—Luke 10:42

Although I am now retired, I have discovered that I have more flexible time than I ever did in the past to serve the Lord. I write daily, teach Sunday school when I can, and preach when I have the opportunity and my health permits. Most of all, I have found that I do a lot of praying for myself and for others, since there are fewer things to distract me from prayer. And I thank God for the opportunity.

Martha was busy preparing food and being a gracious hostess. But Mary was with the men and sitting at Jesus' feet enamored with his every word. When Martha tried to get Jesus to scold Mary for not helping out in the kitchen, Jesus told her that Mary had chosen the better part and he would not allow it to be taken from her.

Preparing the food and graciously receiving guests into your home is important, but cultivating a deeper relationship with Jesus so that you are conscious of his presence, and avail yourself of his strength and guidance is crucial to your spiritual survival.

Prayer: Help me to spend time with you daily in prayer and reflection because that will prepare me to serve and witness to you, as well as help others. Amen.

SUNDAY, MARCH 17, 2013

Read Mark 9:2-13.

A voice spoke from the cloud, "This is my Son, whom I dearly love. Listen to him!"
—*Mark 9:7b*

The first time that the voice spoke from heaven, it embraced Jesus as God's Son in whom God was delighted. This took place at his baptism when the Holy Spirit came down and rested on Jesus, signifying his consistent and continual relationship with the heavenly Father.

On the day that Jesus was transformed in the presence of his disciples, a bright cloud representing the shekinah—or the glory of God—settled on the mountain. Then Elijah and Moses, the epitome of the law and the prophets, suddenly appeared and began talking with Jesus. Not knowing what to say, Peter acknowledged that it was good for them to be there and perhaps they should build three shrines and be prepared to stay there. Then a voice from the cloud spoke once again, affirming the great love that the Father had for the Son and instructing those who were there with Jesus on the mountain to listen to him.

To truly hear Jesus is to understand what he says and also what he wants us to do. The first voice from heaven affirmed Jesus' identity as God's Son. Then the voice from heaven affirmed both Jesus' personhood and his role as Lord: the one who is to be listened to, trusted, and obeyed.

Prayer: Beloved Son of God, let me truly hear and obey your words for me. Amen.

MONDAY, MARCH 18, 2013

Read Mark 10:13-16.

Then he hugged the children and blessed them.
—Mark 10:16

Kaylee addresses me with all the directness that a ten-year-old can muster. She doesn't try to hurt my feelings; she is simply being honest and expresses her opinion from her perspective. Her remarks often give me a reason for reflection.

When the disciples tried to keep the children from Jesus, he "grew angry," and said to them that "God's kingdom belongs to people like these children." Jesus wants us to approach God in a way that is trusting and believing as little children.

Jesus said that to welcome a child in his name is to welcome him—he meant that we need to take seriously the fact that God can speak to us through other people and especially through children. Sometimes the Lord can use a child's imagination, creativity, and directness to get through to us in ways that other adults cannot. Adults should make an effort to spend time with children—talking with them, teaching them, and listening to them. When you learn to appreciate a child's perspective on the world, you will discover a fresh perspective on life. Then God's voice will begin to speak to you in refreshingly new and creative ways.

Prayer: Dear Jesus, help me come to you with the gentle, trusting heart of a child and also listen for your words as they come from the mouths of children. Amen.

TUESDAY, MARCH 19, 2013

Read Luke 9:51-56.

"Lord, you want us to call down fire from heaven to consume them?"
—*Luke 9:54b*

Jesus had a nickname for James and John the sons of Zebedee. He called them "the sons of thunder." While we aren't told the reason for this nickname, we can speculate it was because of their zeal.

Once when they were on their way to Jerusalem, they had entered a Samaritan village to prepare for Jesus' arrival, but the villagers refused to welcome him because they heard that he was on his way to Jerusalem. His destination highlighted the fact that Jews and Samaritans were often in conflict and had different designated places for worship. The Samaritans' lack of hospitality was considered to be extremely rude in that culture. So James and John asked Jesus whether they should call fire down from heaven to consume these uncooperative Samaritans.

It was as if they were asking Jesus, "Do you want us to make lightning strike them and destroy them?" Of course the assumption was that they had the power and authority to do such a thing—power and authority that belonged solely to Jesus. But Jesus "turned and spoke sternly to them." So rather than engage in a tactic of revenge and retaliation, they simply moved on to another village.

Prayer: Whenever I seek to tell others about you, if I am not received warmly, let me not seek revenge against others. Amen.

WEDNESDAY, MARCH 20, 2013

Read Luke 9:37-43.

Everyone was overwhelmed by God's greatness.
—Luke 9:43

When Jesus returned from the mountain where he was transformed before Peter, James, and John, they met a man in the valley who had a son who was subject to epileptic seizures. He had begged the disciples who were already on the scene to liberate his son from this controlling epileptic spirit but, sadly, they could not.

Possibly the reason they had not been effective disciples in the valley was because they had not been on the mountain with Jesus. If we're going to follow Jesus into the valleys and minister to others in his name, then we must also follow Jesus to the mountaintops where he is transformed in our presence and declared by a voice from heaven to be God's Son, the Chosen One, who should be heard and obeyed. Perhaps then we will absorb the power and authority to effectively represent Jesus in the valleys where people are sick and dying and feel overwhelmed and overburdened with the stress and struggles of daily living.

Prayer: Lord, I want to experience your power on the mountaintops of spiritual empowerment so that I will be equipped to serve you and help others in the valleys of despair and defeat. Amen.

THURSDAY, MARCH 21, 2013

Read Matthew 26:26-30

Jesus took bread, blessed it, broke it, and gave it to the disciples and said, "Take and eat. This is my body."
—Matthew 26:26

When Jesus spent his last supper with his disciples, he used portions of that meal, namely the bread and a cup of wine, as a means of explaining the sacrifice that he was soon to make for all of them and for all of us. Each of those who were present ate from the one loaf and drank from the one cup. They each were incorporated into the body of Christ and had a share in the blood of Christ for the forgiveness of sins. They probably could not fully understand the meaning of the tokens of his love that he shared with them on that night, but later on they would understand.

Clearly, Jesus identified himself with the sacrificial lamb of the Passover meal. But he took the two most powerful symbols of Judaism and gave them an even deeper meaning. The bread and the cup no longer provided just sustenance for the physical body. Their spiritual dimension provided sustenance for each participant's spiritual needs. And this observance became a special way of remembering that Jesus was with them always.

Prayer: Lord, whenever I partake of the bread and the cup, give me a fresh experience of your presence as I remember what you have done and continue to do for me. Amen.

FRIDAY, MARCH 22, 2013

Read Matthew 26:31-35.

Then Jesus said to his disciples, "Tonight you will all fall away because of me."
— *Matthew 26:31*

The little boy accidentally knocked the candy dish off the end table. He looked around quickly to see if anybody noticed and then said, "Look what somebody did!" He behaved as if some unknown and perhaps invisible person or persons had rushed through the room and knocked the candy dish on the floor, and now he was as astonished as anyone else at the mess. But someone had seen it happen, and he was made to clean up all of the spilled candy.

Do we really think that we can hide things from God? Most of the time as youngsters, we can't even fool our parents, so how on earth do we think that we can possibly fool God? Adam and Eve tried to hide from God in the bushes in the middle of the garden. After the murder, Cain pretended that he had no idea where his brother Abel was.

Jesus knew his disciples and he also knew that at some point they would all desert him, that Simon Peter would deny him, and Judas Iscariot would betray him. But he continued to give them the opportunity to remain faithful and do the right thing.

Prayer: Lord Jesus, you know me better than I know myself. You know my weaknesses as well as my strengths. Forgive me when I fail you. Help me draw my strength from you. Amen.

SATURDAY, MARCH 23, 2013

Read Matthew 26:36-46.

"Stay here and keep alert with me."
—*Matthew 26:38*

Some temptations are easy to resist while others are more difficult to resist. The temptation that the followers of Jesus faced on the Saturday after he was crucified was a temptation to believe that with his death Jesus' message and ministry had come to an end. He was and is the most beautiful life that ever lived. But when he died on the cross it looked as if that life was over.

The way to resist temptation is not to give in to it. In the garden, Jesus said to the disciples to "stay alert and pray." But they fell asleep. Staying alert suggests self-awareness, knowing ourselves well enough to realize we're grieving over some loss, in despair over broken dreams, or needing time to think through our options and work through our grief over the losses that we have sustained. To pray is to practice Christ-awareness as we seek to enter consciously into the presence of Jesus, drawing strength, direction, and motivation from him. If we stay alert and pray we will be able to successfully resist temptation as it threatens to overwhelm us.

Prayer: O Lord, help me to be aware of my despair and confusion when temptation and despair threaten to overwhelm me. And may I be able to resist temptation with your help. Amen.

SUNDAY, MARCH 24, 2013

Read Matthew 26:69–27:2.

Then [Peter] cursed and swore, "I don't know the man!" At that very moment the rooster crowed.
—Matthew 26:74

In a rural area a neighbor had a rooster that must have gotten its alarm clock mixed up so that it would begin crowing at 1:00 A.M. to welcome the new day. This insistent rooster became quite an annoyance and a point of contention in the community. Eventually, the people who owned the rooster solved the problem by turning it into chicken and dumplings.

One of the tragic notes in the story of Easter has to do with Peter's denial of Jesus. Who when they have read that story has not been able to hear Peter's denial concluded with the rooster's crowing and experience something of Peter's disappointment in himself? And many people every time they see a rooster or hear one crowing think about both Peter's denial of Jesus and the possibility that they too, if they are not careful, might find themselves in a situation where they will also deny Jesus.

Prayer: Lord, forgive me when I make promises to you that I cannot keep, and make me mindful of your forgiveness and the opportunity to begin anew. Amen.

MONDAY, MARCH 25, 2013

Read Matthew 27:3-10.

When Judas, who betrayed Jesus, saw that Jesus was condemned to die, he felt deep regret.
—*Matthew 27:3*

    Things did not turn out the way that Judas anticipated. If his motivation had to do with greed for money, he could find no satisfaction in the silver that he received for betraying Jesus and so he returned it. If he intended to put Jesus in a situation where he would have to use divine power to defend himself and his followers and thereby usher in the kingdom of God ahead of schedule, Judas soon learned that it was Jesus who was in charge of the situation, and he would not allow himself to be manipulated.
    Imagine the deep regret that Judas must have experienced when he heard the false charges and accusations hurled at Jesus and then realized that Jesus had been condemned to die on the cross. Although others would remember him as the person who took the initiative in betraying Jesus, the self-condemnation and loathing that Judas experienced was what eventually did him in.

Prayer: Jesus, help me remember that when I fail you in some way you have already dealt with my sin on the cross. I acknowledge my sin and trust you to forgive me. Amen.

TUESDAY, MARCH 26, 2013

Read Matthew 27:15-26.

"Whom would you like me to release to you, Judas Barabbas or Jesus who is called Christ?"
—*Matthew 27:17b*

Pilate thoroughly examined Jesus and knew that Jesus had done nothing worthy of execution. But Pilate had been entrusted with preserving the peace of Rome at all costs.

He tried washing his hands, symbolically relieving himself of all responsibility for Jesus' fate. Then he remembered the custom of releasing one of the prisoners who was chosen by the crowd during the festival of Passover. So he gave the crowd a choice: Jesus the Christ or Jesus Barabbas. Ironically, both of the prisoners were named Jesus. Jesus was also believed by some to be the Christ or the Messiah. The other Jesus was sometimes known as Bar-Abbas, or son of Abbas. He was probably an insurrectionist and possibly a murderer. It was Jesus the Christ who stood before Pilate to be judged innocent or to be condemned on that day. But on the spiritual level it was Pilate who stood before Jesus on that day to be judged in accordance with whether or not he would choose to risk his position and reputation in order to free Jesus from the travesty of justice in which he had been ensnared.

Prayer: Lord, in response to your having chosen me to be one of your followers, I choose to trust you as my Savior and obey you as my Lord. Amen.

WEDNESDAY, MARCH 27, 2013

Read Matthew 27:32-44.

When they came to a place called Golgotha . . . they crucified [Jesus].
—Matthew 27:33a, 35a

The crucifixion of Jesus took place at a certain time in history when Pilate was governor and at a specific place outside the city of Jerusalem that was referred to as Golgotha, or Skull Place.

The Bible tells us that Jesus was made to carry his cross through the streets of Jerusalem to the place where he was crucified. He had already lost a lot of blood from being scourged with a whip that had many straps attached to it that had pieces of metal or bone on them, designed especially to flay the flesh from the person's back.

We can imagine the scene: the frenzy of the onlookers, some of them excited and others distressed because of the blood that Jesus had already lost. His physical appearance must have made him barely recognizable. Maybe some people cried out for more violence and more bloodshed. Some of Jesus' followers were there and lamented and cried because of the gruesome scene that they witnessed. Some of the soldiers who were charged with carrying out the execution must have been concerned about a riot breaking out that could lead to even greater civil unrest. In fact, the only one who appeared to be in control of the situation was the victim.

Prayer: Savior, when those around me are losing control and the situation itself is getting out of hand, help me keep my thoughts centered in you. Amen.

THURSDAY, MARCH 28, 2013

Read Matthew 27:45-54.

Look, the curtain of the sanctuary was torn in two from top to bottom. The earth shook, the rocks split, and the bodies of many holy people who had died were raised.
—*Matthew 27:51-52*

It can be argued that the crucifixion and resurrection of Jesus are two sides of the same coin composing a pivotal point in human history. This twofold event took place both on earth and in the spiritual realm where the powers of darkness clashed with the powers of light. But although the light can scatter the darkness, the darkness can never overpower the light.

From noon until three in the afternoon, the earth was dark. When Jesus died, the curtain in the sanctuary of the temple that set apart the holy place or inner sanctuary where God's presence was believed to abide was ripped from top to bottom—a symbol of earth being invaded by heaven. The earthquake symbolized that the things upon which the people had relied were now giving way and were no longer reliable. The fact that many of the holy people who had died came out of their tombs and were seen walking the streets of the holy city suggests that temporarily at the death of Jesus, time and eternity overlapped.

Prayer: Lord, through your death and resurrection you make God available to everyone who hungers to experience God's presence. Let your presence become increasingly real to me. Amen.

FRIDAY, MARCH 29, 2013

Read Matthew 27:57-61.

Joseph took the body [of Jesus], wrapped it in a clean linen cloth, and laid it in his own new tomb.
—Matthew 27:59-60a

We know that Joseph must have been a wealthy man because he had a freshly carved tomb that had never been used. Many of the tombs were recycled so that they could be used repeatedly. After dead bodies had been placed in them for a certain length of time, they were essentially reduced to skeletons. Then, the family of the deceased would place the skeleton in an ossuary or bone box that was small enough to be handled by one person and placed on a shelf or ledge, thus taking up less space in the tomb. Joseph could also afford to purchase the costly spices weighing as much as one hundred pounds used in preparing dead bodies for burial. Joseph had such wealth and prominence that he could go to Pilate and get permission to have the body of Jesus removed from the cross and taken to Joseph's new tomb for burial.

Joseph was likely a follower of Jesus who, because of his prominence in the Jewish community, may have kept his relationship with Jesus a secret. He may have had regrets because he did not do more when Jesus was alive to demonstrate his support. Now Joseph could at least demonstrate his love for and support of Jesus with this final gesture.

Prayer: Dear Jesus, help me to realize that it is never too late to show my love and support for you. Amen.

SATURDAY, MARCH 30, 2013

Read Matthew 27:62-66.

Then they went and secured the tomb by sealing the stone and posting the guard.
—*Matthew 27:66*

The Jewish religious leaders went to Pilate and asked him to post guards at the tomb of Jesus, fearing that someone might steal his body. But Pilate told them to use their own temple guards. The guards prevented anyone from getting into the tomb and they posted an official government seal on the tomb making it illegal to open it. This would deter anyone from getting into the tomb or anyone from getting out, for that matter.

But how can you turn back a hurricane with a few soldiers? How do you stop the sun from rising in the morning? How can you protect the world from a miracle—especially the miracle of the Resurrection?

The religious leaders and the guards did what they could. But what they could do was not adequate. Perhaps they began to suspect that something impossible was about to happen, something that the religious structures, cultural expectations, political influence, and military might would be unable to prevent. Perhaps they began to be afraid that they might have been wrong about Jesus and that he really was who he claimed to be. If that were the case, what on earth had they done by opposing him and plotting his death?

Prayer: Lord Jesus, give me true discernment so that I may enlarge the boundaries of my expectations and realize who you truly are and what you can do. Amen.

EASTER SUNDAY, MARCH 31, 2013

Read Matthew 28:1-10.

"Don't be afraid. I know that you're looking for Jesus who was crucified. He isn't here, because he's been raised from the dead, just as he said."
—*Matthew 28:5b–6a*

A large stone had been rolled across the entrance of Jesus' tomb to prevent anyone from getting in. Guards were also posted for a similar reason, and Matthew tells us that a seal was placed on the tomb itself forbidding anyone from tampering with it. But sometime during the night an angel from heaven rolled away the stone. The angel's appearance was so startling that the guards trembled with fear and fainted.

The angel reassured the women who came to the tomb that they had no reason to be afraid. They were looking for Jesus, who had been crucified but was not there because he had been raised from the dead. Then the angel instructed the women to go and tell Jesus' disciples. As they rushed to tell the others the good news, Jesus met them along the way to reassure them of the reality of his presence, to calm their fears, and to tell them to let his disciples know that he would meet them in Galilee.

This was only the beginning of the story that reaches out to us through the centuries and becomes a part of our story too.

Prayer: Lord Jesus, I ask you to step out from the pages of biblical history to be a living and present reality for me, a power and influence at work in my daily life. Amen.